CONTENTS

Words appearing in the text in bold, **like this**, are explained in the glossary.

Look out for these boxes:

WHAT WOULD YOU DO?
Imagine what it would be like to make difficult choices in wartime.

REMEMBERING BRAVERY
Find out about the ways in which we remember courageous acts today.

NUMBER CRUNCHING
Learn the facts and figures about wars and battles.

SECRET HEROES
Find out about the brave individuals who didn't make it into the history books.

INTRODUCTION

Throughout history there have been brave and terrifying stories of escape during wartime. Some of these stories describe leaders and soldiers facing defeat in battle. When all seemed lost, the great generals of history often managed to trick their enemies and escape. In this book you can read about some of the **strategies** and **tactics** that they used.

Capture or kill?

During wartime, the enemy can capture both soldiers and **civilians**. In ancient times, rulers did not bother taking prisoners. They killed their enemies instead. For example, the Aztecs, who ruled an **empire** in Mexico in the 1400s, **sacrificed** prisoners to keep their gods happy. Today, warring sides have agreed to hold captives prisoner rather than kill them. The **Geneva Conventions** set out the international law on how civilians and prisoners of war (POWs) should be treated.

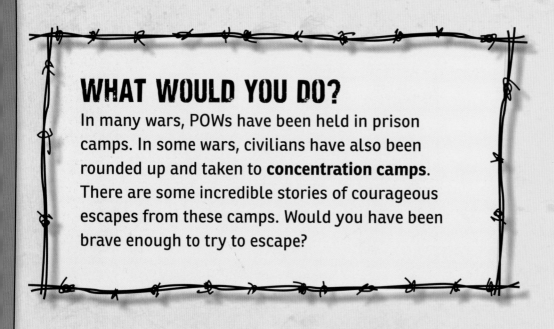

WHAT WOULD YOU DO?

In many wars, POWs have been held in prison camps. In some wars, civilians have also been rounded up and taken to **concentration camps**. There are some incredible stories of courageous escapes from these camps. Would you have been brave enough to try to escape?

WAR STORIES

GREAT ESCAPES

Charlotte Guillain

www.raintreepublishers.co.uk
Visit our website to find out more information about Raintree books.

To order:
☎ Phone 0845 6044371
🖷 Fax +44 (0) 1865 312263
🖳 Email myorders@raintreepublishers.co.uk

Customers from outside the UK please telephone +44 1865 312262

Raintree is an imprint of Capstone Global Library Limited, a company incorporated in England and Wales having its registered office at 7 Pilgrim Street, London, EC4V 6LB – Registered company number: 6695582

Text © Capstone Global Library Limited 2011
First published in hardback in 2011
Paperback edition first published in 2012
The moral rights of the proprietor have been asserted.

Edited by Louise Galpine and Vaarunika Dharmapala
Designed by Clare Webber and Steve Mead
Original illustrations © Capstone Global Library Ltd 2011
Illustrated by KJA-Artists.com
Picture research by Elizabeth Alexander
Originated by Capstone Global Library Ltd
Printed and bound in China by Leo Paper Products Ltd

ISBN 978 1 406 22202 9 (hardback)
15 14 13 12 11
10 9 8 7 6 5 4 3 2 1

ISBN 978 1 406 22210 4 (paperback)
16 15 14 13 12
10 9 8 7 6 5 4 3 2 1

British Library Cataloguing in Publication Data
Guillain, Charlotte.
Great escapes. – (War stories)
904.7-dc22
A full catalogue record for this book is available from the British Library.

Acknowledgements
We would like to thank the following for permission to reproduce photographs: © 2002 Topham Picturepoint p. **18**; Archive Roberto Litvachkes, Buenos Aires/Archive Gerhard H. Ehlers, Odenthal, Germany p. **14**; Corbis pp. **4–5** (Bettmann), **8** (© The Gallery Collection), **10** (© Bettmann), **12–13** (© Medford Historical Society Collection), **25** (© Jacques Pavlovsky/Sygma), **26–27** (© Tim Wimborne/Reuters); Getty Images p. **11** (George Eastman House), **23** (Stan Honda/AFP); Photolibrary p. **22** (Superstock INC); Press Association Images p. **19** (Martyn Hayhow/PA Archive); The Art Archive p. **7** (Musée du Château de Versailles/Gianni Dagli Orti); The Kobal Collection p. **21** (MIRISCH/United Artists); Shutterstock **background design and features** (© oriontrail).

Cover photograph of a silhouette of a man running through a tunnel reproduced with permission of Getty Images (Jac Depczyk/Photographer's Choice).

We would like to thank John Allen Williams for his invaluable help in the preparation of this book.

Stories of courage

Many escape stories have captured people's imagination because of their daring and bravery. Over the years, people have written books and made films about **military** escapes on the battlefield. People also love to hear about prisoners who managed to escape from the enemy and reach freedom.

▼ These Polish prisoners of war were held in a prison camp during World War II.

LEADERS ESCAPING DEFEAT

Before missiles and airstrikes were used in battle, the two sides in a war faced each other close up, on land or at sea. This chapter describes how some great **military** leaders managed to escape defeat and regroup to fight another battle.

Hannibal's escape from Campania

Hannibal (247–183 BC) was the military leader of Carthage, a city in north Africa. Hannibal fought the Romans, who were trying to expand their **empire**. He marched his army to Italy and won several victories. But in 217 BC the Romans trapped Hannibal's army in Campania, in the south-west of Italy. They blocked the mountain passes so Hannibal and his men could not escape. Winter was coming and the Romans seemed to have beaten Hannibal.

► Hannibal's army escaped the Romans in Campania.

Stories say that Hannibal ordered his men to tie burning material to the horns of a herd of cattle. During the night, they drove the cows up one of the mountain passes. The sight frightened the Roman guards so much that they ran away from their posts. Hannibal's army then escaped through the mountain passes. Hannibal went on to defeat a huge Roman army at the battle of Cannae.

REMEMBERING BRAVERY

During the American Revolutionary War (1775–1783), French troops helped the Americans to fight the British. In 1778, the French General Lafayette and his men were spying on British forces at Barren Hill. The British discovered Lafayette and surrounded his camp. Lafayette pretended to attack the British at their rear. Then he and his men quickly escaped down a hidden path to safety. Barren Hill was renamed Lafayette Hill to remember this clever retreat.

► General Lafayette fought in many battles during the American Revolutionary War.

Napoleon crosses the Berezina

Napoleon Bonaparte (1769–1821) was a great French military leader. His army had already won many wars by the time he invaded Russia in 1812. However, this invasion was a disaster. Napoleon's army had to retreat from Moscow, pursued by the Russians. The Russians thought the Berezina River would trap the French. The ice was melting, the water level was rising, and Napoleon's men would not be able to cross. A fierce battle was fought as Napoleon distracted the enemy while his engineers built bridges. Many French soldiers died, but Napoleon and what was left of his army were able to escape back to France.

▼ This painting shows Napoleon marching at the head of his army.

Napoleon escapes from Elba

In 1814, Napoleon was defeated and **exiled** to the island of Elba in the Mediterranean Sea. He escaped from Elba in 1815 and marched to Paris, gathering troops as he went. He briefly took control of France again but Britain and **Prussia** defeated him at the Battle of Waterloo.

This time, he was sent to the island of St Helena, which is thousands of kilometres away. He died there in 1821.

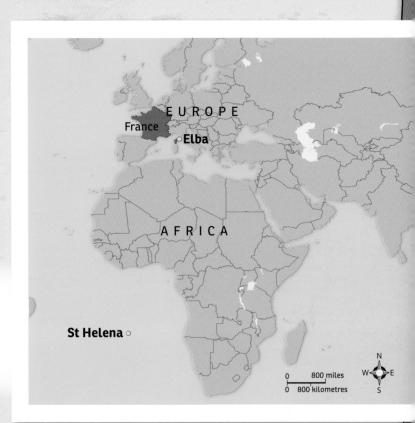

▶ You can see from this map that Elba is very close to France, unlike St Helena.

NUMBER CRUNCHING

The army Napoleon took to Russia in 1812 was possibly the largest that had ever marched in Europe. This grand army was made up of around 611,000 soldiers, from France, Belgium, and Holland, among other countries. Only 50,000 of these men escaped across the river at Berezina and only around 22,000 made it out of Russia.

ESCAPES DURING THE AMERICAN CIVIL WAR

The American **Civil War** took place between 1861 and 1865. Some southern states, known as the **Confederates**, wanted to break away from the rest of the United States, known as the **Union**. One of the issues behind the war was slavery, which still existed in the south.

▼ Many slaves escaped to freedom in the north and fought in the Union army. This is Company E of the Fourth Colored Infantry.

Libby Prison breakout

Prisoners at Libby Prison in Richmond, Virginia were kept in dark, filthy cellars full of rats. In 1864, 109 Union prisoners tunnelled their way out of the prison. They had only a penknife, some chisels, and a piece of rope, but they managed to dig the entire tunnel in just 17 days. They covered it up with dirt and straw until they were ready to escape. Fifty-nine of them reached safety. Forty-eight were captured and sent back to prison.

WHAT WOULD YOU DO?

Many slaves risked their lives to escape to safety in the north. The Underground Railroad was a network of routes, transport, and safe houses where escaped slaves could stay. They were often helped by ex-slaves, who risked being kidnapped and sold back into slavery. Large rewards were offered for the return of slaves on the run. What would you have done? Would you have tried to escape?

▼ Libby Prison was known for its terrible conditions.

Confederate escapes

A daring escape attempt took place at Camp Morton, a Union prison in Indiana. For 12 days in 1863, Confederate prisoners dug a tunnel under the prison fence. They were discovered on the day before they had planned to escape. In the same year, however, 35 prisoners did manage to escape successfully.

By 1864, many Camp Morton inmates had malaria and other diseases. Their situation was getting desperate. One night in November, a group of prisoners ran at the fence, throwing stones and bottles at the guards. They got out into the woods and 31 men escaped. In 1865, a successful tunnel escape took place.

▼ Camp Morton was overcrowded and dirty and it was very cold in winter.

Elmira Prison

Elmira Prison was also a Union prison. Conditions there were so bad that a quarter of all the inmates died. There was only one successful attempt to tunnel out of the prison. The prisoners worked hard to keep their tunnel a secret. They hid the soil they dug up in bags under their shirts and tipped it down the toilet. After digging, they turned their clothes inside out to hide the dirt. They were all sworn to secrecy and had agreed that they would kill anyone who betrayed them. Despite all this, the guards were suspicious and tortured one man for information. In the end, 10 Confederate men escaped to freedom.

NUMBER CRUNCHING

Elmira Prison was open from May 1864 to July 1865. During that time:

- over 12,000 prisoners were kept there
- there were 793 cases of **scurvy**
- 2,963 prisoners died of disease and malnutrition
- 17 prisoners escaped.

PRISONERS OF WAR IN WORLD WAR I

World War I (1914–1918) was started by rivalry between powerful countries in Europe. Old **empires** such as Britain felt threatened by expanding countries such as Germany. Britain, France, Belgium, and Russia fought against Germany and its supporters. Soldiers from many countries around the world, including Australia, India, the Caribbean, and Canada, fought with the British. The United States did not join the war until 1917. Both sides fought terrible battles and many prisoners of war were captured.

SECRET HEROES

After World War I, people wanted to remember the dead soldiers whose bodies could not be identified. Monuments called The Tomb of the Unknown Warrior were built in many countries. People visit the monuments to remember the **sacrifice** these soldiers made.

▲ The German pilot Gunther Plüschow was a prisoner of war during World War I.

German journey

In 1914, the British captured the German pilot Gunther Plüschow in China. He escaped and boarded a ship to the United States, which was not yet in the war. He pretended to be ill so that anyone searching the ship would not come too close.

From San Francisco, Plüschow travelled overland to New York, where he boarded a ship to Italy. The ship stopped at Gibraltar, where the British captured him. He was taken to a camp in Britain, from where he escaped during a storm. Plüschow disguised himself as a sailor and sneaked on to a ship going to Holland. When he finally arrived home, the Germans thought he was a spy! He was eventually rewarded and became a hero for his daring escape.

▼ This map shows how Gunther Plüschow's escape took him halfway around the world.

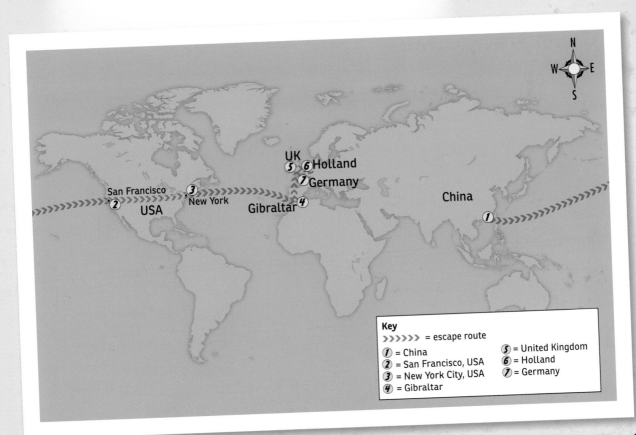

Key

>>>>> = escape route

1 = China
2 = San Francisco, USA
3 = New York City, USA
4 = Gibraltar
5 = United Kingdom
6 = Holland
7 = Germany

The Escaping Club

Many prisoners of war tried to escape over and over again. In 1916, the Germans thought they had found a solution. They put all these men together in a very secure prison known as Fort 9 at Ingolstadt, in Germany.

However, the plan backfired. The prisoners shared their experiences of escaping from other camps and gave each other lots of ideas. Escape attempts from Fort 9 took place at least once a week! These attempts failed, but when the prisoners were moved to another location by train, two soldiers jumped out and got away. Their names were Evans and Buckley. Evans later wrote a book called *The Escaping Club*.

Close to freedom

Tommy Henderson was a British soldier who fought in the Battle of the Somme in France. People at home thought Henderson had been killed. In fact, he was in a prison camp in Germany, where the prisoners were made to work in mines. Henderson and two friends hid in a mine lift shaft until they could run away. They walked to the Dutch border but were captured before they could get to safety. Henderson was taken back to the camp where he stayed until the end of the war.

WHAT WOULD YOU DO?

Prisoners could not get much information about the war. Some prisoners thought that the only way to survive was to try to escape. Others thought it was safer to stay in the camp and hope that their side would win the war soon. What would you have done?

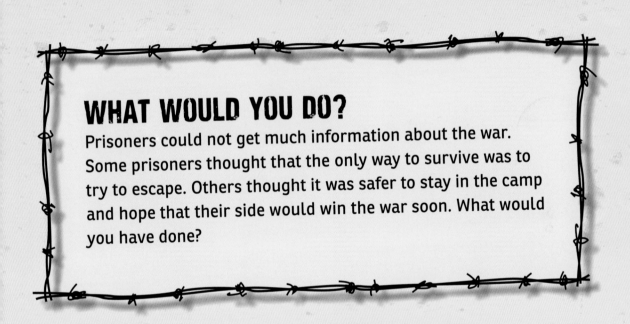

◄ Evans and Buckley leap to freedom from the train.

GREAT ESCAPES OF WORLD WAR II

After World War I, Germany was poor and weak. The **Nazi** leader, Adolf Hitler, became popular by making Germany strong and powerful again. Germany allied with Italy and Japan and began invading other countries. This led to World War II (1939–1945). **Military** personnel and **civilians** were taken prisoner around the world. Some managed to escape to freedom.

Colditz

Prisoners who tried to escape many times were sent to Colditz Castle in Germany. It was supposed to be escape-proof, but that did not stop the prisoners trying. A British officer named Airey Neave and a Dutch officer named Tony Luteyn made their own German uniforms and walked out of the camp in full view of the guards! Another British officer, Peter Allan, hid in an old mattress that was being dumped. He got out of Colditz and made it as far as Vienna before he was recaptured and sent back to the castle.

▲ Franz von Werra was a German pilot who was imprisoned in Britain and tried to escape several times. Once he disguised himself as a Dutch pilot and had climbed into an RAF plane before he was recaptured.

NUMBER CRUNCHING

British, American, and French prisoners were not treated as badly as the nearly 6 million **Red Army** soldiers captured by the Germans. Only around 2 million of them survived. Japan treated British, American, and Australian POWs badly and only about 60 per cent of these prisoners survived.

▼ In 1945, some prisoners built a glider to try to escape from Colditz Castle, but they did not succeed. This photograph shows these former prisoners with a modern model of their glider.

The wooden horse

Some of the most famous stories of prisoners of war escaping took place at a German camp in Poland called Stalag Luft III. This camp was for air force personnel from a range of countries, including Britain, Australia, and the United States.

Many escape attempts were tried, including the use of a wooden vaulting horse (a piece of equipment used for gymnastics training). One man would hide inside the horse and dig a tunnel near the fence, while the others exercised. The soil was hidden in bags hung inside the horse. Eventually three men escaped down the tunnel to freedom.

The Great Escape

In March 1944, another legendary escape was made from Stalag Luft III. This time 76 officers got out through another tunnel. It was the biggest escape from a prison camp at the time.

The prisoners had made their own compasses and **forged** travel and identity papers. They made civilian clothes and fake German uniforms for the escapees to wear. An American prisoner organized a choir to sing and cover up the noise of the loudest work. However, almost all of the escaped men were recaptured, with only three making it safely to Britain.

REMEMBERING BRAVERY

Over the years, stories of prisoners escaping from enemy camps have become famous. People love to hear about true tales of bravery and many books have been written describing these events. Escape stories also make exciting films. In 1963, a film called *The Great Escape* was made, telling the story of Stalag Luft III and the men who tried to escape.

▼ The men imprisoned in camps such as Stalag Luft III were watched closely by guards at all times to prevent escape attempts.

Escape from horror

During World War II there were other prison camps known as **concentration camps**. The Nazi leader of Germany, Adolf Hitler, had these camps built so that certain groups of people could be rounded up and killed. These included Jewish people, Romany gypsies, and disabled people. Millions of people were murdered in these camps during the **Holocaust**. Those who survived suffered terribly and the stories of those who escaped are **inspiring**.

▼ These children were imprisoned in a camp at Auschwitz, in Poland, during the 1940s. The striped clothing they are wearing was the prison uniform.

Out of Auschwitz

More than one million people died in the concentration camp at Auschwitz. They were either killed by the Nazis or died from disease and malnutrition. Alfred Wetzler and Rudolf Vrba managed to escape. They hid under a woodpile for four days before escaping through a hole in the camp fence.

When they escaped, Wetzler and Vrba took a plan of the camp with them showing the **gas chambers** where people were murdered, as well as a label from a can of the poisonous gas used. This evidence helped to stop thousands of Hungarian Jews being taken to the camps and made the rest of the world aware of what was happening there.

Jan Karski, a Polish man who fought against the Nazis, ▲ helped Jews and other **refugees** escape during the war. He became a hero for his efforts.

REMEMBERING BRAVERY

We remember the millions of people who died in the Holocaust on Holocaust Memorial Day. This takes place on 27 January, which was the date in 1945 that the camp at Auschwitz was **liberated**. It is important for people to remember those who suffered and died so these terrible things will not happen again.

CIVILIAN ESCAPES IN WARTIME

Wherever a war takes place, it is not only the **military** who face danger. The **civilian** population in a war zone can suffer terribly and often people face huge risks to escape death. Sometimes people are forced away from their homes and become **refugees** in a strange place.

The Vietnamese boat people

The Vietnam War took place from 1955 to 1975. **Communist** North Vietnam was fighting against South Vietnam, which was supported by the United States and other countries. As many as 4 million Vietnamese people were killed. When communist forces finally took over in the south, many fled from their homeland.

Thousands of Vietnamese boarded boats, hoping to be rescued in international waters or to reach safe countries such as Malaysia or Thailand. The unlucky ones were stranded at sea for days in unsafe boats without food or water. Many fell victim to pirates and other criminals. Eventually, many boat people were put in refugee camps or resettled in other countries. Some returned home when life became safer but thousands remained abroad.

REMEMBERING BRAVERY

The Vietnam Veterans Memorial in Washington, DC in the United States was created to remember members of the US armed forces who died fighting in Vietnam. The Memorial Wall has the names of all those killed or missing written on it. The wall was designed by the artist Maya Lin.

▼ These Vietnamese refugees were prevented from coming ashore in Malaysia, so they had to travel further on to a small Indonesian island.

CONCLUSION

Today, most wars are fought in a way that means there may not be many more stories of daring escapes. In modern warfare, each side often tries to make targeted strikes on the enemy. There are not as many prisoners of war taken as in the past.

Sometimes **civilians** are captured and used as **human shields**, to stop the enemy attacking. When prisoners or hostages are captured in this way it can be very hard for them to escape. They often remain imprisoned until they are released or killed.

Remember refugees

Sadly, wars will always force civilians to leave their homes and flee from the fighting. **Refugees** from various conflicts all have their own stories of escape to tell. It is important that they have a chance to tell their stories so that people around the world understand and remember that wars are still tearing people's lives apart today.

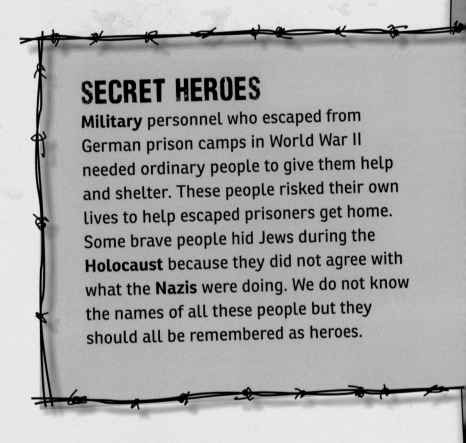

SECRET HEROES

Military personnel who escaped from German prison camps in World War II needed ordinary people to give them help and shelter. These people risked their own lives to help escaped prisoners get home. Some brave people hid Jews during the **Holocaust** because they did not agree with what the **Nazis** were doing. We do not know the names of all these people but they should all be remembered as heroes.

◄ Troops working in Afghanistan face the daily threat of hidden roadside bombs. Specially trained bomb-disposal experts work hard to help them escape this danger.

GREAT ESCAPES AROUND THE WORLD

USA
General Lafayette outwitted the British at the Battle of Barren Hill in Pennsylvania. The hill was renamed Lafayette Hill to remember him.

USA
Libby Prison was in Richmond, Virginia. More **Civil War** battles were fought in Virginia than in any other state.

POLAND
Some of the worst **Nazi** death camps were in Poland, such as Auschwitz, Chelmno, and Treblinka. Stalag Luft III was also in Poland.

GERMANY
Germany's aggressive behaviour was a major cause of both world wars. Prisons such as Fort 9 at Ingolstadt and Castle Colditz were in Germany.

BELARUS
Napoleon lost many men at the Battle of Berezina. The troops who survived had to endure a long journey home to France.

CHINA
Gunther Plüschow was shot down in China in World War I. He was based at a German colony and was fighting against the Japanese, who wanted to take the colony and other land in China.

VIETNAM
The Vietnam War ended in 1975, when the communist forces took control of Saigon in South Vietnam. The new government then imprisoned many people from the south or sent them to special camps.

GIBRALTAR
Gunther Plüschow was captured by the British on Gibraltar, a peninsula off the coast of Spain.

TUNISIA
Hannibal was a **military** leader in Carthage, which is now part of Tunisia in north Africa. The city of Carthage was rich and powerful and eventually became part of the Roman Empire.

IRAQ
The first Gulf War took place from 1990 to 1991. A second Gulf War, also known as the Iraq war, began in 2003. Saddam Hussein was removed from power but the war has caused ongoing problems in the region.

ITALY
Hannibal led his army to Italy and fought the Romans in several battles. The Romans trapped him in Campania but he used his military skill to escape.

GLOSSARY

civil war war between different groups of people within the same country

civilian ordinary person who is not part of the military

communist system of government where one party controls what goods are produced in a country

concentration camp prison camp in which the Nazis held people under terrible conditions, until they died or were killed

Confederate one of the southern states in the United States that wanted to break away and form their own government in the 1800s

empire large number of countries ruled by one country

exile forced to live away from your own country

forge create false documents

gas chamber specially made building in a concentration camp where the Nazis killed people with poison gas

Geneva Conventions series of international treaties that aim to protect soldiers and civilians in war

Holocaust mass killing of European Jews by the Nazis during World War II

human shield civilian hostage who is placed in a location to prevent the enemy targeting it

inspire give encouragement and hope to others

liberate set free

military to do with the armed forces

Nazi ruling party of Germany from 1933 to 1945, or a member of it. The Nazis were led by Adolf Hitler.

Prussia kingdom in northern Europe that was made up of lands that are now in Germany and Poland

Red Army army of the Soviet Union

refugee person who has had to flee their own country to find safety

sacrifice offer people or animals to the gods by killing them. Also, when a soldier gives up his or her life for the nation.

scurvy disease caused by lack of Vitamin C, that involves bleeding under the skin and teeth falling out

strategy careful plan or method

tactic action carefully planned to achieve a goal

Union states that made up the United States after some southern states tried to set up their own government in the 1800s

FIND OUT MORE

Books
Non-fiction

Difficult and Dangerous: Desperate Escapes, Simon Lewis (Franklin Watts, 2009)

Give Me Shelter: An Asylum Seeker Anthology, Tony Bradman (Francis Lincoln, 2007)

Global Issues: Refugees, Cath Senker (Wayland, 2008)

Fiction

The Boy in the Striped Pyjamas, John Boyne (David Fickling, 2010)

Websites

www.napoleon.org/en/kids/index.asp
On this website about Napoleon Bonaparte and his family, you will not only find lots of great information, but also games, quizzes, maps, and timelines.

www.bbc.co.uk/schools/worldwarone
You can read and listen to the stories of people who lived through World War I on this website.

www.bbc.co.uk/schools/primaryhistory/world_war2
The BBC Primary History website has lots of information about World War II.

A place to visit

The Imperial War Museum
Lambeth Road
London
SE1 6HZ
www.iwm.org.uk

Visit the Imperial War Museum to learn more about the wars discussed in this book.

INDEX